# Life Is
# NOT
# What You Think

## Permission to Go Out of Your Mind

Rob Reider

Life Is Not what You Think:

Permission to Go Out of Your Mind

By Rob Reider

www.CoachPresence.com

Line editing and design by Estelle Slootmaker

Photography by Joey Schultz (cover) and
John Hanson (Mr. Reider)

ISBN-13: 978-1974258611

# Foreword

## *LIFE IS NOT WHAT YOU THINK*

*Sometimes we get sidetracked as to what we are supposed be doing in this lifetime. Rob's book shows us how to get back on the main road. There are many who learn the message of their Masters but few have the endurance and patience to spread it to the world. Rob's book is a monument of experiences and love. He has an uncompromising gift of distilling and integrating the mystical teachings of his Masters and bringing them to life. This book is not just philosophy but draws on a foundation of experience so that it is insightful, penetrating and practical enough to bring profound shifts and transformative processes into everyday life.*

*With Love and Blessings,*
*Yogi Amrit Desai*

# Acknowledgments

I want to thank Leonard T. Reider, Kathleen Powell, Aaron Reider and Natalie Reider for their guidance and support. They are the world to me.

So many clients, students, friends, and strangers I have met have asked for a simple yet profound guide to living dynamically. It is the recognition of the presence of something so great that no word could ever describe the actuality that has led to the unfolding of this document and these practices.

I am grateful for the kind loving help of Estelle Slootmaker, Andrea Reider, Max Lockwood and "all that is" for organizing the data for this adventure.

I am also grateful and humbled to experience the love from my teachers and Masters: Master Ja Fu, Master Yen Hoa Ly (Lee), Krishnamurti, Swami Amrit Desai, Swami Chidvilasananda (Guru Mayi), Mata Amritanandamayi (Amma), Mirabai Devi, Sifu Kam Yuen, David Hawkins, Adyashanti, Marcel Marceau, Tom Leabhart and Tony Montanaro.

*Let the adventure begin!*

*A basic principle is:*
*Energy flows where attention*
*goes. If your attention is caught*
*up in conflicting, dualistic mode*
*of the rational mind then your*
*energy is divided at the core.*

— Amrit Desai

# Table of Contents

*To Be or Not to Be?*

*That is the Question!*

—William Shakespeare

No, it's not.

# Introduction

$\mathcal{A}$wakening to the truth of life is very interesting. On the one hand, you have the extraordinary experience and loving juice that the universe musters up within the physiology. On the other, you may realize that the ego's thought-based promise of enlightenment does not deliver. In fact, you get quite an ordinary, extraordinary result. When you find that a non-dualistic, non-separated result is all that is left, you wonder what all the struggle was about. It was on such a day that this story unfolded for me.

In December 2003, while vacationing in California, I decided to do multiple Yoga Nidras, a form of guided, deep rest. Because, in the past, I studied and spent time with Shaktipat Masters and Chi Masters, I had become very sensitive to energy. This particular time, a surge of energy traveled up my spine and out the top of my head.

After the Yoga Nidra was done, I sat up. Life had a different feel, but I could not describe it. I hiked up a mountain trail.

I found that colors and sounds were nearly neon, bright and full. Even so, I still felt a "me" separate from the nature I was walking in. As I proceeded up the mountain, I contemplated a stress that was in my life, and then followed the contemplation with a Ramana Maharshi recommendation, "to whom has this thought arisen, *who am I?*."
Instantly, a flash — the brain showed all of life as an epic journey of humankind. I felt overwhelmed by love. Uncontrollable tears and sobbing overtook me. All that was — was no longer outside of me. There was no me. Just a unified non-duality, anchored in love. It came instantly with knowingness, spontaneity, and abilities in touch healing. I lost all fear, as there was no Rob to have fear.

> *One good move is better than ten thousand bad moves.*
> —Yen Hoa Ly

The overwhelming bliss of living had replaced separation and the need to dominate. Life revealed itself as a dynamic, continual change without time or space. Oneness without a now. No over-there, because there was no over-here.

My teacher, Yen Hoa Ly, used to say, "One good move is better than ten thousand bad moves."

Thinking, conceptualizing, and depending on mental constructs add up to more than ten thousand bad moves.

As we explore beyond conceptual life, we become sensitive to life itself. A new, pronounced sense of love, awe, and innocence unfolds. This appreciation of life itself, this great teacher, offers a diverse approach to aligning yourself to your true nature, your natural self.

\*\*\*

$\mathcal{T}$houghts cannot lead you to this dynamic outcome. It is dynamic because it is ever changing; thought forms and labels always lag behind the actuality. Thoughts (words, labels, ideas, concepts) are always 1/100,000th of a second behind reality. (This is an approximate measurement. Notice something and measure your timing, if you require data or are a scientific genius.) Words work great for ordering food, but they do not fill the belly. Together, you and I will discover truth in action and feel our wonderment.

*Find life experiences and swallow them whole. Travel. Meet many people. Go down some dead ends and explore dark alleys. TRY EVERYTHING. Exhaust yourself in the glorious pursuit of life.*

—Laurence K. Fish

This book maps a path along which you may experience insight. Efficiency and simplicity are often the best formats for absorbing, transforming, and creating a path for understanding yourself. Your natural self. Your unlimited self. That-which-all-things-occur-through self.

These pages will help you explore the life that allows you to integrate your experiences. Everyone's life is full of integrated experiences that they pay no attention to — for example, what the sky looked like on the third Tuesday of last month. In other words, many of life's experiences and thoughts pass right through and, therefore, in a sense are integrated. The source of all lies within. What lies within is all that you can see, hear, feel, and think — the whole universe, in fact. This book helps you explore your mind and seek the answer to this question: "What the heck is going on in there?"

So, with a light heart, fasten the cosmic seatbelt and allow your natural abilities to play together on the playground of life — simply to enjoy the pure joy of your experience on this earthly plane. Even if it doesn't always feel good, life is change and change is how we experience the immediate world and the rest of the shooting match. Everything is in — all thoughts, ideas, and occurrences everywhere and every now.

## Reflections

*The lunatic is in my mind and it's NOT me.*

— Pink Floyd

# 1

## Life Exists —

## apart from Your Thoughts.

ife is not what you think. Nature exists without your thoughts about it. Yet, thinking occurs in life. Thinking is the ability to represent multiple ideas about life. I am not trying to convince you of anything, but urging you to inquire for yourself. To that end, and to begin the discovery of truth, you may have to explore the regions that consciousness brings you to.

I am not placing any value on thinking, rather, just noting that it occurs. What you need to explore is this: Can there be something going on that you aren't aware of? Are you like a fish in the sea that can't find the water? Are you so used to thinking about life that you wonder where life is? Are you walking down slippery slopes? Are you happy? Are you living a fulfilled life? Or are you asking — as when God contemplated suicide — "Is this all there is?"

Out of this mess, we create a society and a culture of measurement, comparison, and false pretentious behavior. The result is people pleasing, party worshipping, and divided religious communities, each more self-righteous than the next. Now, if you are divided in your own non-sense of self, and so is someone else, you might fight each other. You might try to control each other. Some of us might even try to control another country. After all we can impose democracy (promise of freedom) and end up with yet another economic enslavement.

What a nightmare. We have lost our sensitivity to ourselves and therefore to each other. We think we have freedom but this is not freedom. Freedom to use a credit card, debit card or checkbook is not freedom. It is not awareness from whence all joy comes.

There is no end to the rapacious nature of humankind operating in a non-integrated state. An integrated idea, thought, or mental concept dissolves like the breath comes and goes without holding on. Something nonintegrated appears over and over in our consciousness — triggered by some event or words.

The good news? You do not have to renounce anything, in the religious sense. You don't have to do one more thing — trust me you have done enough. If the behaviors, patterns, and experiences of your life are not working, you can modify them by going directly to their author and change the program — switch out the old tape. You can upgrade! You don't have to defragment your consciousness. Rather, you can explore the territory in a way that naturally allows these items to fall away, like shadows disappear in the presence of light. But, you must ask: What is modified, who is the modifier, and who am I?

> The greater understanding
> is that "life is" — all of it.

Your thoughts may arise from indoctrination or because you simply assume something to be true. Once locked into the brain's labeling system, these thoughts engender a sense of separation from life and, often, desperation. Is there life beyond the limits of thoughts? The greater understanding is that "life is"— all of it. Change appears on this fluid existence, a oneness of life, and, in that, thinking happens as well.

The intrinsic value and the pull of desire and resistance associated with thought about something, will create the effect. At the end of this convoluted process comes judgment. Our judgments can contain the same words but with very different meanings. For instance, the phrase, "I'm at the end of my rope." This sounds like a very negative association. But, what if you are hanging on for dear life off the edge of a cliff? You would joyously reach for the end of your rope, welcome anyone throwing it to you, and be truly thankful for being pulled to safety. Essentially, how much you identify with or argue against the thought, idea, or concept, determines how far down the rabbit hole you are willing to go. In other words, your attachment to the outcome dictates your identification with an idea.

> How do you start?
>
> Of course at the very beginning —
> the feel of life itself,
> untouched by thought.

When riding the ride of yet another virtual reality — after all it is only occurring inside our heads — you start connecting nonexistent dots and writing new stories — creative visualization of the mundane.  You see, we are hard-wired to our emotional body. Everything feels real, whether it is or not.

\*\*\*

$\mathcal{T}$ he end result of putting these practices in place is to undo the momentum of your mind. Not to only smell the roses, but to realize the essential nature of you, the rose, and all that is.

How do you start? Of course at the very beginning — the feel of life itself, untouched by thought. You see, it is occurring anyway. We might begin to venture into the mechanics of consciousness and recognize that the focus of our mind, our attention to something for any reason, is the usual operating status. What if you can simultaneously see and feel without touching or looking? What if you can realize that your nature and nature itself are not different?

The OMG experience of this recognition can bring the heartiest of egos to its knees. No control necessary. Control was only an idea that created a false security anyway, like most stories we tell each other. Chaos would be too much for our fragile ego, and yet ... the absoluteness of life exists without a thought about it. The beloved.

If you want to feel the connection that is there, get off that train you are riding. It is on a collision course with sorrow and suffering. It will bring down the ship, the captain, the crew — life wasted, and for what? Control? What are you afraid of? The only reason to control is to avoid this fear. Is it the big kahuna in disguise? Fear of death?

Please let your ego go — after all it's just another idea. If you let go of this concept of "me" (the persistent ego), your life's possibilities become unlimited in every moment. In other words, please die to your ego and live forever.

It is hard to imagine that any folding into ourselves is selfish. Any projection onto anyone or event is selfish, not in the normal sense of the word but more of a "me-centered" activity. It is one big selfish ride. It cannot be about anyone else if it is going through the same old filters. Life is thinking, "Well, that's a horse of a different color."

So, let's continue to explore this idea of "me," the trap it sets, and how quickly it does it.

# Exercise

One of my favorite books is by Bob Adamson. Its title says it all: "What's wrong with right now, unless you think about it?" Test the waters right now.

◊ Casually observe the sights and sounds of the present moment. Relax with your gaze. With innocence and appreciation, notice the world around you — miraculous in some eyes —and through you.

◊ Now, think about something you want to get done, or something that bugs you.

◊ Feel the difference between present moment awareness and thinking.

As you explore this elusive phenomenon of actuality versus conceptuality, you will see that thinking encourages more thinking. This only leads to continual construction of a virtual reality with all the justifications and personifications that go with it. Stay in it long enough and you just keep inventing another idea of yourself and, then, something you have to do. It is that continual motion, like a mouse on a wheel that keeps us practicing empty rituals and looking for love in all the wrong places. How can you get to Detroit if you keep driving to Chicago? This is the ultimate derailment that traps you in patterns and disconnects you from the source of joy, love, and freedom, which is your birthright.

# Reflections

*What's wrong with right now, unless you think about it?*

—"Sailor" Bob Adamson

# 2

# Be with What Is as Is ... or Suffer

Quintessential to living life as presence is understanding that how you perceive creates your world. You must understand what interferes with a direct experience of awareness or presence. You have an endless ability to mentally sort experiences with your master labeling system. Your judgments follow along, labeling experiences with a charge of desire or resistance and creating what appears to be reality. This happens in such a split second that you believe it is real. Alas, for many it is as real as it gets. As Buddha said, life is suffering. This quick play — of processing direct experience through mental, emotional, and psychological filters — is the source of the suffering.

In biblical language, we could say Adam was expelled from the garden when he took the bite of the apple, which represents knowledge (labels).

Let's get down to it. As you examine life in any given moment, you must remember that life includes all of life, not just your personal, segmented thinking but also everyone else's segmented thinking. If you throw in a dash of identification with a self-righteous edge to it, you have a vast separation from presence into the depth of filters with no end to that rabbit hole.

Do you get the problem in the first place? How can any idea, concept, or thought ever be what is real? Take a step back and relax. You have a thinking mind that likes to sort. Why let a sorting mechanism live your life? You see, in all of its sorting, it cannot grasp the totality of life. You may have a righteous mind. But, simultaneously, people are committing heinous crimes all over the world that you didn't even pick up in your radar of thought or control. These relentless assumptions are really imagined.

How is it that we let so much go? How is it we can let ourselves go after creating the most heinous crime against ourselves? The mind is violent to itself when it imposes labels and judgments instead of seeing. Knowledge, accumulated in all its forms, can keep us from experiencing the real. A bite into the apple of knowledge leads to an immediate expulsion from the garden of presence. It just seems such a step down and such a letdown.

As the masses now effectively confuse essential living with pretentious living, we give way to the programmers, whose deep understanding of controlling others creates the dependency on TV, religion, so-called education, and the other effective indoctrinating devices — infatuation with movie stars, TV programs, and continual idiotic forms of conversations that repeat that which is never present. These are all placebos for living, not real life. Crap in, crap out, and the wheel of sorrow continues. Stop yourself now!

Without stopping the momentum — a full stop — we will continue as before.

\*\*\*

Take a step back and see what the heck is going on. See if you can be with what is, as is, without trying to modify yourself, others, or the event. Take a moment and let that sink in. Step back to widen your gaze, and take notice from the full spectrum of your brain. Relax into all areas of the brain and notice life around you. Let the judgments go and just watch. Observe the flow of life, which may include the flow of thoughts. As they arise, let them flow through your mind like clouds passing over the deep blue-appearing sky, like images on a mirror or a movie projected onto the silver screen.

Take more time, and as you do, you may find that things have always been coming and going. The breath comes and goes. People come and go. The seasons come and go. Food comes and goes. Bodily sensations come and go. Life could be defined by the comings and goings on an emotional level or physical level, but these are always tagged with emotional attachments and identifications. Eventually, though, the intensity of the event fades and it settles with all the rest of the memories.

\*\*\*

How can you do this thing called being alive without all the kicking and screaming? How can you stop from doing great bodily harm to yourself and others? Beliefs affect the physiology. Let go of certain beliefs and your body chemistry also is set free. How can you flow with grace and presence and meet each moment with sensitivity — not the walking-on-eggshell type of sensitivity? Real sensitivity meets each moment with intelligence.

Essential action results from awareness acting alone, not in the crowded house of identities trying to be right through one-upmanship. We are actually experts at this already. We let so much of the wholeness of life go. The focus of our attention, plus a positive or negative charge, creates the persona with its reactions. Instead, turn your attention to being with what is as is.

> *Real sensitivity meets each moment with intelligence.*

What do you know? How is it you know something? What if you take your labels off all things and see what you know now? Can you know how honey tastes by the words describing it? The taste of an apple? The word is not the experience. You see how convoluted this may be. By backing off from taking a position on everything, you can create a real relationship with yourself, others, events, and all that is in the world around you. Seeing the world as it is — is effortless.

Conversely, it requires great effort to impose your judgments or labels onto the object, person, or situation. As you do this, the object becomes a subject with your imposition of judgment. You then become the judgment and the world "exists" as you describe it with prejudice. Old tree, tall tree, bad tree, good tree, tree — these descriptors become programmed in the mind. You lose the real and substitute a word or set of words.

These descriptors work for communicating with others. For understanding and being with what is — to make effective changes in your life — you must let them go. By suspending judgment from the subject, you see the object. New life occurs. Insight comes pouring in. Leave the judgments for the television fundamentalists and pundits and their mind-corrupting patterns.

\*\*\*

With honest inquiry, you find the root of judgment and labeling to be a ritual dance from the past. These reference points are quick shots of a past — learned behaviors triggered by the present situation. Some of these are "moves from the crib" that cry out "hold me," "feed me," "pay attention to me," "listen to me." You may have learned other labels and judgments as socially acceptable or protective patterns.

> By backing off from taking a position on everything, you can create a real relationship with yourself, others, events, and all that is in the world around you.

These judgments and labels only serve to harm you and separate you from the deeper connection you already have. We are nature. Yes, from the dressing to the programming, we are nature. We contain thoughts, yet we are not those thoughts. We are nature. The hidden treasure that lies beneath all that dressing is an unlimited field for play. Instead of trying to be like someone, just be — and enjoy the ride. It doesn't require any effort to be. It is your birthright.

> We contain thoughts, yet
> we are not those thoughts.

Your thoughts are like clouds that come and go. As a child, perhaps you made patterns with them. You saw a dog, a mountain, or another shape that matched some idea in your head. By its very nature, the cloud dissolved and shape-shifted into something else. You have the same capacity with your thoughts. You can shape-shift circumstances to align with a certain outcome.

Usually, on the negative side of things, we roll them into a formula for self-deprecating talk. The past conditions get triggered with new events as you perceive them and voila, you are in total react mode. For example, in the past, a dog bit you. Now, every time you see a dog you panic. Instead, why not go back to what your mind was just before that thought-shape came in? As Bob Adamson asks, "What's wrong with right now unless you think about it?"

# Exercise

◊    Remember a time you flowed with the situation.

◊    Reflect on a time when everything was "just right."

◊    Recall a time when the more you did, the worse things got.

◊    Contemplate a time when you fully appreciated someone or something for what it was.

◊    Remember a time when someone appreciated you for just being you.

◊    Reflect on a time when you witnessed something in nature and it was breathtaking.

# Reflections

*It's hard to come to grips with the fact that our own interpretation determines the effects that anything will have on our internal state.*

—Peter Ralston

# 3

## You Are Creating Your Own Life.

## Why Not Create It Differently?

*P*lease note! You are a powerful creator. You have not been doing anything by yourself. You are being supported and sustained by all that is, that actually brought you to this point in your life. Just imagine if the trees (and the oxygen they produce) weren't here, let alone all the other events that make up your now. So, you can use the mind to create the desired outcome. You feel this with all your heart. When done, a feeling will arise (e.g., satisfaction, relief, joy). Feeling this, you then want to express this outcome of the feeling (you see yourself celebrating, sharing, joyfully living, etc.).

The joy of creating any outcome is the play of consciousness. You use your vivid imagination and harness the love of your heart, which, in turn, aligns with and creates an already fulfilled desire.

When you look closer, you see that you do this with negative thoughts, too. You project an undesirable outcome and then feel the end result. Judge, jury, and executioner are happy to take center stage of your mind and thwart your heart's desires.

> *You use your vivid imagination and harness the love of your heart, which, in turn, aligns with and creates an already fulfilled desire.*

Understanding how the mind works will free even the most foolhardy skeptics. After all, they are doing it as they are being skeptical. Get it?

\*\*\*

The key to creating your heart's desire is to harness the feeling that having it brings you. When you use that feeling, really connect to that feeling, you can use it any time to reset yourself.

Do not get caught in the particulars of how the solution will appear. Stay with the feeling. When your mind picks up on any negative idea about anything pertaining to your outcome, bounce back to your new uplifting feeling. Bounce and you will feel the joy in your heart. Bounce and you will change how you feel, see, and hear. Let go and let the universe align with this feeling. Miracles are about to happen.

Start with something that is a true heart's desire. Stick with this and make it so. Bounce to the feeling as often as possible. You will really enjoy being uplifted in this way. Do this often for the rest of your new life. Do not be surprised if people come to you and say, "What have you been doing?" Or "What's new? You look different. You look happy and fulfilled."

When you are ready for your next heart's desire, enjoy it as the next reality in your life.

This is how dreams come true. This is a living dream in alignment. Do not worry about the particulars. The opportunities to act will reveal themselves. Do it now!

# Exercise

Create. Create. Create. You are anyway.

Neville Goddard has shaped many people in the self-empowerment world. His astute recognition of life through the mind portal gave way to many courses on the popular scene, renamed and reworded to hide the fact that the source of these insights was Neville. Nonetheless, this creating exercise is a reminder of how we tend to experience most thought forms.

Use the four steps listed below. Imagine, feel the outcome, and turn back to that feeling often. Go for it. The more relaxed you are, the better the outcome.

1. From your heart's desire, create with your mind, as if it was done, the ideal situation you would like to have happen in your life.
2. Feel it as if it was so. Make it an absolute reality in your mind. Completed.
3. Next, if that is so, how does it make you feel?
4. And finally, with that feeling, what might you do with your life? How would you express yourself?
   (For example, if you felt happy you might do the happy dance.)

*I have realized that the past and future are real illusions, that they exist in the present, which is what there is and all there is.*

—Alan Watts

# Do It Now.

o it now. This quintessential lesson allows you to be free of you, without limits — pure action versus a constant play of reaction.

You've heard about "being in the zone." It seems as soon as you notice it, you lose it. You see you can't do both. In the zone, you learn lessons and complete great tasks without the usual mental limits you place on yourself. After all, do you constantly tell yourself to breathe, to blink your eyes, or to pulse your blood? In reality, life simply occurs. You may notice that you're breathing or blinking, but you don't rely upon an emotional, psychological identity to make those actions happen. Your life becomes less complicated if you relieve yourself (or some idea of yourself) of the responsibilities of running command central.

Do it now. Action occurs in nature without something claiming responsibility. The tree does not say to the leaf, "time to drop or else." Nor, does the wind claim responsibility for blowing. When you really stop to consider this lesson, you may realize that most of your day is done without your authorship. When you get caught up in thinking, you miss the life that is occurring.

Humans often react out of fear. When fear is your motivating factor, you consider this action or that action to be essential for your survival. Your judgment about a situation creates urgency — and you begin your yo-yo ride on the mental-chatter roller coaster. You spiral into a web of authorship, importance, necessity, and survival. You engage in being "right" as your moral duty. You may even engage others to listen, do, and join your cause. Suffering is sure to follow. You may finish the task, but at what cost?

When you really get honest, you realize that being right at the cost of feeling contentment and love is a pitiful substitute. When you live yet another sold-out ramification, it will have its play and effect in consciousness. Then, out of some new necessity, you create another task — endless list of tasks, endless emptiness trying to get fulfilled. Like overeating can cause obesity in the body, over-thinking, having to control and having to be right can cause obesity of the mind.

*P*eople who are caught up in this mental trap have repellent, outrageous, outward, harmful reactions that never stop, no matter who gets in the way. When you buy into this downward mental spiral, you may lash out at those you love the most. After all, according to your scheming, they are in the wrong. Attach enough self-importance, and you might even do great bodily harm to anyone who does not believe the way you do.

One simple key unlocks this mental trap — love. Love is the space that allows for all things, including change. Change continually occurs anyway. Night naturally gives way to day and so forth and so on. Random acts of kindness can teach us a simple lesson: action can be its own fruit. Let go of the idea of you. It's just an idea. Notice that life flows, like brushing your teeth, tying your shoes, or driving a car.

> *One simple key unlocks this mental trap — love.*

Most humans have too much self-importance. This leads to control issues (and we are not in control to begin with). What is the inherent fear that lies underneath? Who has done you wrong? What are you trying to prove? Who are you trying to get approval from? Your boss? Your spouse? Your father? Your mother? Your lover? The boogieman? When you get stuck in this play, you live in reaction. Repeating the thoughts you've heard from others and fulfilling their expectations will lead you to a life of disappointment.

\*\*\*

What if you allow yourself to just do an action? If thought comes in, other than the voice of integrity as an ethical built-in barometer, you set the thought aside and just take action. When you commit to action, life unfolds as the teacher. If you feel you need to adjust from the action you took, then you will.

Conversely, by holding back until you have the perfect amount of control, the perfect idea of perfect, the perfect scenario, the perfect you who cannot make mistakes (the you who is judge, jury, and executioner), before you have a chance to actually do anything, you may find great regret and remorse for your empty life as life has passed you by. Or, perhaps you live life with an "at least" mentality. For example, "I don't have a job but at least I have a car."

Do you take actions because they live up to someone else's idea of what you should be? Can you see how this leads to an empty shell of non-fulfillment?

\*\*\*

You can't do life wrong; it is the great adjuster. It flows with you and supports you in mysterious ways. Ours is a "yes" universe. Life allows you to fall from your perceived grace and lovingly holds you in its true grace.

Muster up the courage to face your fears, your insecurities, your scenarios of what you think perfect is. Dust off that bucket list. Really live. Recheck that to-do list. Perhaps rename it the "to be" list. Breathe. You are okay — you always have been. You have the power to let it rip. Do it now. Dance like no one is watching. Feel the gratitude of life itself for life itself.

Your thinking, controlling, scheming brain can't make this happen. When you abandon the idea of you, you can turn your attention to the miracle of life that is unfolding right now! It is easy. It is natural! It is you as you have always been.

I remember when my own father was in the process of dying. He said, "I feel exactly as I did when I was four." He got that right. Awareness operating through you is timeless, ageless, loving, and non-judgmental. You do not need any authority figure to tell you that you are alive. You have universal energy running through you, sustaining your life.

You need no permission slip; your birth gave you that. Let go, just a little or a lot, and dive in. Do it now. Do not look for the grade report from a teacher or peer. Do not look for a college degree to give you permission to feel okay. Do not look for anyone, including your idea of yourself, to give you your life. You are, therefore you are.

> Let go, just a little or a lot, and dive in. Do it now.

Failure is not you. You can't fail at being you. Behavior is an option, and so is learning. You can learn, grow, and change behaviors. You do not need an identity to brush your teeth — or to do anything else. You have the right to express any action, just don't limit yourself to the calculated outcome.

Do it now. Be the action required in this new moment. Pour yourself into the action you want to express as. Abandon the thinking and go for it. You will be amazed at the freedom and passion that will fill you and excite others. Do it now!

# Exercise

◊     Recall a time when you just took action without thought.

◊     Remember a time when thinking interfered with action.

◊     Recall a time when you over-thought actions you were going to take.

◊     Consider the times in your day where thinking is not occurring, but action is completed.

◊     Ask yourself who is the voice in your head that sounds like you. Could it be a conglomerate of patterns, programs, identities, or your parent's voice?

*Enlightenment is a destructive process. It has nothing to do with becoming better or being happier. Enlightenment is the crumbling away of untruth. It's seeing through the facade of pretense. It's the complete eradication of everything we imagined to be true.*

— Adyashanti

# 5

# The Master Remote

hen it comes to choosing the programs your mind is playing, you control the master remote. You have the ability to change channels. In other words, you can shift your attention from drama or angst to a more pleasant experience — or not.

For instance, let's call the way you feel about a certain perceived problem Channel Three. For example, "The people I work with are so insensitive." On your drive to work, you tune into Channel Three. As you think about how insensitive the people you work with are, you get you all riled up on the inside — and you won't be seeing any of them for yet another half an hour. Take a hold of that master remote and change the channel.  Simply put your attention on a better feeling — relief is just a click away. Consider the love that you have for your partner or children or some accomplishment. Call this Channel Eight. Just as you would with a TV remote, shift your attention to a new subject.

This practice shows you that the power of dynamic living is the ability to shift your attention. Do you remember, as a child, having fun playing with friends and effortlessly changing from one play idea to the next? You did it just because it was fun. Maybe you got tired of the last game you were playing. You moved from one fun activity to the next, effortlessly and with enthusiasm.

\*\*\*

*A*dults become far too serious because they identify too stringently with their beliefs. It's hard to resist the programs that our beliefs have patterned. They are so ingrained that it's like they have hijacked our nervous system and emotional body. Nonetheless, beliefs are only an idea. You can change ideas or programs or channels because you are the creator and source of those things.

It is funny, though. As you practice changing the channel and shifting your attention, it is quite possible that problems you perceive will resolve. You see, a myopic viewpoint captures only a small segment of life as you see it. A whole lot more is going on in the universe. If there were no trees, there would be no we. It is a yes universe that will gladly support your ideas of anything.

You can gather evidence to support any idea. It wasn't too far back in the history of the earth that people swore that the Earth was flat. Maps proved it. The actual did not. Press your remote and shift your attention. You will feel better — much relief will come your way.

> Nonetheless, beliefs are only an idea. You can change ideas or programs or channels because you are the creator and source of those things.

# Exercise

◊    Think about a time when you were able to shift your attention.

◊    What is your Channel 3? How does it serve you to stay tuned into it?

◊    What is your Channel 8? How does it make you feel?

◊    That time you shifted your attention ... how did you manage to do so?

◊    Can you apply that action and take back control of your master remote next time Channel 3 starts to play?

*Love is a flame without smoke,*
*ever fresh, creative and joyous.*

— J. Krishnamurti

# 6

## The Cravings: I Want Some

*L*et's look at one of life's common denominators. Plants do it. Animals do it. Humans do it. All are in a constant state of craving. Cravings are instinctual. At cellular levels, all living things crave what keeps them alive. Except for aquatic creatures, most living beings crave water. You could say that craving is a natural outcome of being alive. It's not that instinctual craving is a problem. For example, eating is necessary.

The problem arises when the craving becomes psychological and, of course, emotional. This leads to suffering. When the psychological/emotional body gets hold of a craving and demands that it shows up, cravings become their own brand of twisted. Consider cravings for fast food, designer clothes, or all the substances fostering addictions. This is not to say any of those things are bad or wrong. However, in the play of consciousness, not having your cravings fulfilled can leave you feeling "less than."

*O*ften, religion, politics, materialism, and insensitive educational systems cater to the mind's emotional cravings, leading people down a path to dependency rather than empowerment. These systems, and others like them, fold into themselves and do not offer true fulfillment. The wrapping is better than the gift.

Without fulfillment and a sense of love in your heart, you look to the outside — to objects, people, coffee, alcohol, or drugs. You substitute an idea about something for the genuine, natural bliss that is waiting for your discovery. Maybe you crave to be enlightened. Or, you crave your yoga class. You talk like you are spiritual. You modify another idea of yourself that creates identities to fulfill yet another craving to get accepted. It's a big mess.

\*\*\*

*S*ociety, as a macro image of the individual, continues to feed the masses. We take it hook, line, and sinker. The media feeds it and there appears to be no end to the greed promoting it. This wholesale slaughter of the masses is being spoon-fed one addiction at a time. It gets so insidious that your adult life feels dependent on how the digits of your retirement account are climbing. A dip in the market and you are off to the races with judgments of gloom and doom.

We crave safety for the future. We crave acceptance for the past. We crave forgiveness. We crave our paycheck. We crave a new car. We crave, crave, crave!

The ego has its own language for cravings. It goes something like "If I do, get, have this, then ... (fill in the blank)." It's a race to the future that holds you hostage to an idea that cannot satisfy you for long. It cannot satisfy for long because before you blink, it is on to the next craved object. The monkey mind falls for it again. The craving sets in like a vampire in search for blood. People are unhappy with themselves so they think objects or goals will rescue them. I am sorry to say that if you have been unhappy all of your life, the word "retirement" may not save you from those unhappy beliefs. You might want to reevaluate the source of happy and unhappy.

\*\*\*

Cravings come hand in hand with control. We feel this nasty craving or desire; then plot to control the universe; and enroll others to try to achieve this superficial satisfaction. This no-win situation is what frustrated lives are filled with. The wheel of sorrow continues to roll. With that, we pass our social patterns and limited thinking on to our children — and really anyone who will have us.

Our craving is the focus of our attention. But what if, while all that is going on, something else is not craving. Look out at an object, any object, in the room or space where you are right now. Focus your attention on the object. This is what happens in your thinking. You focus your attention on your thoughts.

> Witness all of it and step out of the cravings that keep you small.

Now, back to your attention on the object. Notice that, like a camera lens, your vision really sees much more than what you are focusing on. There is a witness taking it all in, without comment and without craving. You are the field for all that is happening. Witness all of it and step out of the cravings that keep you small. It's a rush to feel the limits fade away and the juice of the universe fill your soul. And, it will settle well with your friends. They will appreciate you much more than when you were an addict or crusader.

Crave not.

# Exercise

◊   Recall a time when you craved something. How did it
    affect you?

◊   Reflect on how the craving affected you. Was it a
    physical, mental, emotional, or psychological craving?

◊   Remember how you felt from satisfying the craving.

◊   Consider how you felt when you did not satisfy the
    craving.

◊   Recall somebody else's behavior when they were
    craving something.

◊   Consider whether satisfying these cravings brought
    fulfillment on a deep level or a superficial level.

◊   Note and contemplate whether you were watching the
    craver (the craver within yourself).

# Reflections

*There is much unexplored potential in each human being. We are not just flesh and bone or an amalgamation of conditionings. If this were so, our future on this planet would not be very bright. But there is infinitely more to life, and each passionate being who dares to explore beyond the fragmentary and superficial into the mystery of totality helps all humanity perceive what it is to be fully human.* —Vimala Thakar

# 7

# Sleight of Mind

*I*t's important to look at why problem areas pop up and then focus on them. We must look at the root of the problem itself. It has been introduced to the mind as a problem. Why?

Why is this the problem that bothers you rather than the senseless killing and destruction happening somewhere in the world? Why do you accept that authorities are practicing wholesale slaughter? Why not focus on that?

You have tuned-out real issues going on in the world and instead have focused on a problem that is a threat to your self-image. The ingredients of the problem have been tailored by your mind to protect and defend a false self-image. You drum up the past and code it, in this present problem, as a new real issue.

> Let go of that idea and live
> as if it wasn't there. You
> are the magician ...

Look closely and ask yourself if you have ever felt this way before. It won't take too long to discover that the problem is just a new recipe for the same old thing. Let go of the old thing and the new problem quickly vanishes. Let go of that idea and live as if it wasn't there. You are the magician; you executed a masterful sleight of hand. Now with the new feeling and freedom, what's next?

Now what?

Go for it!

# Exercise

Put your mind on something that seems to bother you. As you delve into the problem, from your mind's eye, see where the problem shows up.

◊    Is it in your belly or in your mind?

◊    Is there a feeling associated with this thought or idea?

◊    Does it have legs to the past?

Just watch the mind. In all the areas, it seems to go with the thought form. Ask yourself: "Under all the circumstances, is this the way it really is?"

◊    Is this the truth or is it just the way you see it?

◊    Remember, this is a representation of a problem installed by you. Is it possible you got it wrong?

◊    If someone else looked at the problem idea, would they think the same thing?

Now imagine that the problem just wasn't there.

◊ What would you feel like if it just wasn't there?

◊ What is your life like now that it isn't there? You simply suspend it in your mind.

◊ Notice how this makes you feel. Does it create space for you to see the problem from a different viewpoint?

Practice on a variety of issues you think are problems, one at a time. Notice how it affects you when you simply pretend that the problem isn't there. Put it outside of yourself. Just set it aside like the world problems you set aside.

◊ What would your life be like?

◊ What qualities would it have?

Practice this and you will nicely lighten up and create room for resolution.

*"There is a vitality, a life force, an energy, a quickening, that is translated through you into action and because there is only one you in all time, this expression is unique."*

— Martha Graham

# 8

## My Greatest Addiction Is Me

*T*hou shalt have no other image before me.

Oops, but what about me? My greatest addiction is me.

\*\*\*

*Y*ou've heard the saying, "Wherever you go, there you are." But what about following that up with: "Who am I?"

Of all the practices to find the self, Ramana Maharishi has said that the most important is to inquire into the source of your thoughts. What a profound experience — to find the source of the thought of me, the field where all of life occurs. This recognition of self can lead to an unlimited experience. This non-dualistic, unifying occurrence lies at the source of all of life. It is so profound that a "me" cannot contain it. It is all of life itself. One cannot even imagine it.

Yet as the idea of a "me" subsides, this otherness occurs. It's always there waiting, non-temporal, without dimension, without separation from anything. It operates as love and is the glue of the universe.

\*\*\*

*A*s a basis for existence, a relationship occurs, chaotic as it is, that operates and co-mingles with the phenomenal, while never losing sight of the noumenal. This relationship is based in love and respect for all that is. Only with this perspective of knowingness can you realize the fundamental importance of sensitivity to the world in its entirety. Sensitivity here does not mean the sense of being afraid of being hurt. Rather, it speaks to an aware state that sees, feels, and acts in accordance with the demands of the moment. Your actions are in accordance with the situation that is before you.

We could call the noumenal the "I am" experience, or the self. It is being-ness or is-ness. We could call anything that follows the words "I am" as the doing or the doer (e.g., I am shopping, I am running, I am parenting, etc.). The very act of doing with identification can limit the flow of boundless creativity and fulfillment that each moment can provide.

> Listening to the world without filters of personal doer-ship creates a palette of possibilities.

With sensitivity, you act without personal doer-ship but with perfect action, as is required. Your response and responsibility match the requirements that each situation presents. Otherwise, you bring your past to the table and push an agenda that simply doesn't fit. You must, without moralistic pre-judgment, find the appropriate response.

Listening to the world without filters of personal doer-ship creates a palette of possibilities. You listen to the sound of a bird without judgment. You listen to your partner without judgment, and this helps you feel where they are coming from. Perhaps as you listen, you sense that what they are saying is not as relevant as how they are saying it. This art of communication requires stepping aside from your initial reaction and finding the depth, the hidden message.

\*\*\*

This is the Art of Presence — the experience of each moment without labeling, judging, reacting, or doing. Life through you informs you, and action happens. Communication becomes convoluted when identities are performing through individuals. You must ask questions to explore the presentation. What is this identity demanding? Investigate it with sincerity. The same must happen with your own identity. What does it want? More often than not, it is the equivalent of a move from the crib.

A baby communicates when he is not getting what he wants, needs attention, needs a change of diaper, and so on. Adults are trying to communicate their needs and wants, too. If only adults would change the diaper in their mind — lots of crap up there. Questions will lead to the truth behind the demand. But first, you have to listen.

$\mathcal{H}$ow can you listen with the utmost attention? If, when someone is speaking, you instantly refer back to your own experiences, then you have taken your attention away from the person speaking. You have now self -reflected and made it about you. It appears that most conversations go this way. They are based on reactions rather than real thought.

\*\*\*

$\mathcal{F}$or example, if someone says "black," the response is usually "white." Your past programming kicks in and associative memory takes you down a familiar path. As that happens, you also lose your ability to listen and perceive the real message being delivered by the person speaking. It becomes a "me" ride instead of a "we" ride.

Who, then, is this "me"? A conglomerate of past, accumulated thoughts? We call this normal communication — it is most people's status quo. What would happen if you could walk away from a conversation totally inspired and feel like you were really listened to, that a new perspective or insight could come in to solve a life dilemma? Would that be a conversation worth engaging in? It would no longer strengthen the "me" but would connect with a "we." We all win when one wins.

> Live in this and new life comes to you ... You feel the hugeness of each moment.

Let the "me" go by the wayside. Let the dead bury the dead. This insidious self-image with all its implications only serves to separate you from all of life. As you begin to connect with your unimpeded sensorial world, you begin the glorious journey into the miraculous life. Your "me" cup is emptied to make room for the "we." The gentle breeze is felt, the laughter of a child, the sound of a bird — even the sorrow that calls for your response.

Live in this and new life comes to you. You connect to events, people, and places with a real presence. You feel the hugeness of each moment. You no longer have to shrink to a virtual me, which is rigid and limited. The excitement of every new now welcomes you.

# Exercise

◊   Recall a time when your idea of yourself was limited by judgments about yourself.

◊   Remember a time when your idea of yourself and life were too small to include the rest of life.

◊   Recall a time when life seemed bigger than you.

◊   Remember a time when your idea of yourself did not match what you really felt about yourself or your potential.

◊   Reflect on who this "me" is that you refer to.

◊   Contemplate whether the idea of a "me" is another thought, and, if you are not a thought, then who are you?

# Reflections

*Revolution, total revolution, implies experimenting with the impossible. And when an individual takes a step in the direction of the new, the impossible, the whole human race travels through that individual.*

—Vimala Thakar

# 9

## Help! The Tree Has Hold of Me!

*A*s prevalent as thinking is, it is not uncommon for the mind to occasionally capture and hold a willing participant hostage. Humans are naive. As I have said before, to want or to not want something requires attention and energy. The root of resistance is the resistance, not the change or the subject. In other words, what we resist is the resistance, not so much the feeling. Yet, even though foolhardy, we are all in and swallowed up by a belief, which, by the way, creates a believer.

The believer is, once again, an identity, not yourself. One easy way to get caught is to compare yourself to another or hang on to a pre-described goal or ideal. When you do this, you work with the devil himself, well, in all those details.

Measurement and comparison are fantastic ways to create self-loathing. This, or any other hook, gets us to hold on and even defend our attachments. On the other hand, being with what is "as is" is presence, untouched. Wanting or wishing something to be different than it is creates space for dissatisfaction and can allow some pretty destructive patterns to emerge.

What if, while relaxing the judgment, you see the truth and accept the right-now as where you are. Demands would decrease, imposed stresses would soften, and you would realize that this pattern of never being good enough is a pattern indoctrinated by society. After all, the idea of original sin achieves this and creates a world of believers who consistently and willingly live their lives feeling "not good enough."

> Don't be for or against it, just entertain it. Take it for a ride. Then let it subside — and see what's possible.

hy do only certain thoughts hang us up? What is invested in the profile of that thought? What else is attached to that thought? What other thoughts or fears may be lying in the background?

Ultimately, fear lies at the root of our getting hung-up. You fear getting hurt in all its forms. You fear not being approved of or not being liked. You feel the pressure of having to show up as a liked identity and then not getting approval or acceptance, not getting what you want, trying to control, wanting to be controlled, not wanting to be controlled, and on and on. Some people dominate others in conversations thinking that if they are "right," they gain something.

This pretentious behavior and unnatural pattern create a momentum. When anything challenges this protocol, you get hung up — from issues as mundane as which flavor of ice cream to pick to those as serious as suicide. Here is a great time to plug this truth: KILL YOUR EGO, not your body. Go with the flow. Accept each idea that comes in your mind as if you invited it in. Just entertain it. Don't be for or against it, just entertain it. Take it for a ride. Then let it subside — and see what's possible in this new now.

*P*erhaps, in the gap of not reacting to the idea, you become informed of new possibilities and new pathways of opportunity. This is somewhat like Einstein's power nap, during which he said ideas came to him. Let go of the resistance and choose for yourself. It is not about being right. It is more about the flow of life itself. Choose and take action. Choose and handle the new arrangement. Choose and empower yourself to the unknown. Choose and let love flow from your heart. Choose and co-create the next moment's adventure.

This does not mean you cannot dream of a goal or create an intention. It means that you do it from a very loving space by harnessing the god-like creational abilities we all have. This is a game changer if you want to create something different for yourself.

> You can let it go nicely and remind yourself, "That was then, this is now."

The very latching onto an idea creates a governor on our creative problem solving. You are a receiver. You are the field for all existence. As such, thoughts come through this very fine tuned instrument. Ideas universally flow throughout all and you pick up on them. They are not "yours." They just are. You, then, can share them without ownership. You can let them come and go with great ease.

Holding onto re-creating some idea of pain or pleasure is just an expression of your idea of the past. You can let it go nicely and remind yourself, "That was then, this is now." If you just didn't have that thought, what would be there? What would the situation or person be like if you let that one go? It is amazing that when you let it go, what remains is appreciation of the rest of life.

# Exercise

◊   Recall when you were consumed by an idea or belief. Is
     it still there now? What changed?


◊   Consider what the gain or win was for holding
     that idea.


◊   Remember the fear that led you to hold on so dearly to
     this idea.


◊   Contemplate what ideas are worth holding onto, even
     though they cause you to become limited.

*If someone offers you an amazing*

*opportunity and you're not sure*

*you can do it, say yes —*

*then learn how to do it later.*

— Richard Branson

# 10

## From Me to We

hat do you really do? How do you really show up? You have to have a higher purpose. That will be our reason to work together today, so you can explore "What is your why?" You have to find a why to do it for your own reasons.

When you have a big why — a strong reason for why you do something, you ignite somebody else's why. What is your why? Why do you show up? Who do you show up for? What do you really want in the highest level of your being? When you move from your why, not from your what, you can move with passion.

\*\*\*

y *why* has always been, every day, to help somebody else. Why? Because, I have discovered that this is a "we" world. So, every day, I go out of my way to help someone. My why is to put someone before me, because there is no separation. We are all in this together.

When a healthcare practitioner can say, "My why is to have the power to help others take charge of their health when they feel helpless and hopeless," they will see more fruit from their labors than a colleague hung up on the patient data and his practice's bottom line.

A sales person, no matter what their attitude, behavior, or skill set, will not succeed if they believe that money is the root of all evil. But, if their "why" is to bring blessings to customers with the product they are selling, they will find their zone and sales success.

> My why is to put someone before me, because there is no separation. We are all in

Some beliefs that derail us are apparent; others are transparent. That is, you don't know that you have a belief going on, and that it's sabotaging your business, relationships, and life experience. So, yes, you are your own worst enemy. And, you are also your own greatest cheerleader.

What I'd like to do, to help you move from me to we, is to understand how your mind works. First, think about "identity" versus "role." Another word for identity is thought. Thoughts about yourself. Negative stuff comes in here. This is the last thing you want to share with people. Instead, play your role. Show up playing the role that the person you are with is demanding. Become sensitive again. (If you don't ask some questions, you'll never find out their why. Move from your heart, and people will tell you about themselves.)

Next, look at programming. Here's an example of programming: I say "black" and you say "white." You jump to these associative memories and then babble your stuff to someone else, and think you're relating to them. This is the root cause of suffering in relationships.

Here's another example: I say, "I'm too warm" and another person says, "I'm not." I am thinking, "I don't give a crap. I am thinking about me." There is no sensitivity. The other person could have asked, "Oh, is there something I could do for you?" Instead, we both jump into our own world and immediately shut down the relationship. In truth, when less of "me" happens, more "we" happens, and we really start connecting with each other. So, move from your heart and start asking people questions.

> People want to be listened to, understood, and appreciated. When you practice active listening, move from your heart and connect to somebody else's words.

Finally, become an active listener. Active listening is the ability to listen to what somebody says and repeat it back to them, so that they see that you are listening to them. It's a remarkable skill. People want to be listened to, understood, and appreciated. When you practice active listening, move from your heart and connect to somebody else's words. Have a good conversation about what is important to them, and if they need help, help them.

If you find yourself over-thinking, stop it, and move into pure action. When you move into pure action, it's like being in the zone. Action does not require thinking.

Life is change, like it or not. At any given moment, it's already changing, and you are the focal point of all the change that's occurring in the world. See, it is you that is the universe that's occurring.

# Exercise

**Ground yourself.**

You can use this nice little exercise at all times. There is never a time that you would not want to be grounded. Thinking in excess is a very un-grounding experience. Over-thinking and nervousness can cause one to feel more agitated and less present. Grounding stabilizes you in your environment and easily creates being present in situations.

Grounding is the basis for showing up fully present. Spinning up into your brain (mind) leads to an uncomfortable experience that spirals you into more thought-spinning experiences. In the sense of Yin and Yang, this is a very Yin, out-of-balance condition. Grounding will help you neutralize yourself in all situations.

◊   If standing or walking, imagine or pretend that your feet have roots. Imagine or pretend that your feet are weighted to the ground. Imagine or pretend that water flows downward from your feet. Imagine or pretend that as you walk your feet are anchored with each step. Imagine or pretend that your feet are heavy.

◊   If sitting, imagine or pretend that you are weighted in your seat. Imagine or pretend that your bottom is weighted to your seat. Imagine or pretend that you are anchored to your seat. Imagine or pretend that wherever you are, you and the surroundings are anchored to the Earth.

*Give up honor and pride, give up love of body. Only then can you see God everywhere and in every being.*

— Nityananda

# 11

## Your Highest Expression

*L*et's look at universal principles. They have inspired world change. They have brought governments and institutions to their knees. These principles respect and dignify life.

These principles have inspired millions of people, at the heart level, to live with purpose and dignity. They have forged the bond at a core level, which is the foundation of relationships based solely on love. It is encapsulated in the essential words of our Declaration of Independence, "We the people." It is witnessed when we observe the loving exchange of a mother and child gazing into each other's eyes.

Our hearts soar and action aligns when our call to life comes from inspiration and passion. When we move from compassion with each other, we are elevated to our highest expression.

People rush to aid us in our quest to help others. This is natural. This is effortless. These are the bonds of a shared experience.

These are the calls to action of an inspired people. These are the results when there is no compromise on basic human expression.

We are life. We are nature. We have to respect nature or we destroy ourselves. Get It. We are not separate from nature; we are human nature. In all areas. Undeniably, biologically.

> Put aside the "what's in it for me" and replace it with "we."

Together we will look into our inner compass. We will need to know for ourselves, not the speaker, if we have integrity. Can we respect others and ourselves, by listening to our inner compass? Is who we associate with in alignment with the efforts of all or the few? We will explore not the "what" we have today, but the "why."

When we put aside the "what's in it for me" and replace it with WE, we can all win in a mutually agreeable and beneficial way.

\*\*\*

*L*et us examine what inspires us at our deepest level. We will suspend the ideas of the past. We will not impose our ideas of the future. We will explore this now, this why, and this purpose that has brought us together.

As we move forward in any given now, we will use our creational powers to inspire and guide others to theirs. Otherwise, we drag people through an agenda that, at the least, is not inspiring and, at worst, may be detrimental. We need to connect to our why so people can move to theirs.

\*\*\*

*W*e are in a life of relationship. The world, so to speak, has gotten smaller. Although we function in a world economy, each person comes from a very different past. The way we perceive the world may be different. We must not push our agenda but, with respect, seek the truth and meet the demand that is required — not as a challenge, rather with sensitivity.

---

# Life is a contact sport.

---

We must dial down the me and make room for the we. We need to listen better, talk less, and perhaps give up on being self-righteous.

Life is a contact sport. Sharing is not one-sided. We must listen to what is said by observing their posture and the feeling behind their words— the unspoken.

Find out the other's emotional reasons for wanting a change in their life. Allow them to feel where they are coming from; then, you can better understand them. It is magic to connect with someone in such an intimate way — more intimate than putting something inside your body.

Food, that is.

Food becomes our blood. That's intimate. It becomes our life source. It affects how we show up in the world. So do words. They go straight in, whether they are yours or others. They affect your chemistry and become all that you are. The greatest discipline is mastering what goes in and out of your mouth. Speak with love. Speak with the other in mind. Speak as if their heart were your own, because it is.

Stand up and show the world that you made a difference for yourself — and, that you have made a difference for other people. We don't often see the effects we have on others. We must share this experience — not hold back.

Take comfortable steps and uncomfortable steps to put someone else before you. Do they have concerns about their health? Their finances? Their body image? Their respective family members?

You will never know the impact that you have on the rest of the world. You can only control you. So let go of fear and share from your heart. The rest will go the way it will go. This is the way.

The commercials on TV from the big pharmaceutical companies have people worried that they might wake up depressed and need more toxins in their bodies. What they really need, in many cases, is good food. Malnutrition can show up as inflammation, disease, emotional bankruptcy, mental exhaustion, physical challenges, or being at the brink psychologically.

> Don't let your ideas about the world get in the way of your journey. After all, you are not your ideas.

Our whole society also suffers from malnutrition when it comes to integrity. We are the tail wagging the dog. However, WE, the people, with rekindled dignity and integrity and an inspired vision, can show up differently. This is our collective journey.

Don't let your ideas about the world get in the way of your journey. After all, you are not your ideas; you have ideas. They will change from time to time.

# Reflections

*If we want to understand life, to know
of death, peace, love, we have to step
away, go beyond the conditioned
realm of mental movements and dive
in silence, into complete relaxation of
the conditioned mental movement.*

— Vimala Thakar

# 12

## Let It Rip. Let It Go. Speak Your Why.

Do not let your ideas about your self-worth, body image, or any other comparison to another person stop you from sharing from an inspired place. Be the why, your passion for helping others, or touching others in a significant way. Be the light that drives you. We affect people we have never met. We create new life where the hopeless stood.

We may not know who they are, but they are you in another form: Someone who may have had a challenge in their life, someone who wants to get healthy and live again, someone who needs a new conversation about health and wealth, someone who is crying on the inside with despair, someone who didn't know it could be this easy.

> Be the light that
> drives you.

When we hold back for any reason — don't introduce ourselves to someone, fail to bring up our opportunity, do not speak up, do not voice our concern, do not challenge someone to do better — then we fail as humans and become selfish. That's right: It becomes all about you and by not sharing you become selfish.

Let it rip. Let it go. Speak your why.

You must have a higher purpose. Do it for the love of your children, humanity, and the precious Mother Earth. It's not what you do. It is why you do it. It's not what you've got. It's what you do with what you've got. Be the change you want to see in the world. Gandhi influenced millions of people. Lead by example.

Quality of life has no price. We are all going to die one day. What we are asking you to do is live. Live a high-quality life. Live in alignment with your greater purpose and you won't age. Live in alignment with your greater purpose and abundance will follow. Live in alignment with your greater purpose and your relationships will have deeper meaning.

It is infectious to live in a creational moment-to-moment way. Step up to the challenges in life. There are many. However, you have been built by the Creator to not only handle these but also to soar. Fly high. Abandon your old thoughts. They are dead. They are useless. Let go of the damaging patterns. You will know which ones they are because they feel like a bummer.

Live in alignment with your greater purpose, forge a bond with your fellow humans and live happily the rest of your days.

> Live in alignment with your greater purpose, forge a bond with your fellow humans and live happily the rest of your days.

# Reflections

Since 1970, Rob Reider has been actively engaged in many holistic health modalities—as a student, teacher, guide and practitioner.

Since his first reading and time spent with Krishnamurti, Rob was set on a path to understand the nature of consciousness. His continual dedication to studies with Masters from China and India led to a remarkable understanding of non-dualism and an energetic expression of living.

Rob now coaches, inspires, and mentors others to awaken from dogma and programming to an unlimited possibility of living. The essence of these ideas is expressed in this book. Rob helps others live and perform in a "peak" experience, calling his work "The Art of Presence."

Learn more at www.CoachPresence.com.

67954145R00066

Made in the USA
Lexington, KY
27 September 2017